Covenant and Fire

Covenant and Fire
Rekindling the Vow, Restoring the Flame

Kirk Juetten

ByteCoreMedia

Safety & Abuse Note

A Note on Safety and Honor

Marriage is holy.

But holiness never excuses harm.

This book calls husbands to bleed and wives to trust because Christ bled and the Church trusts.

That beauty never legitimizes abuse of any kind.

Headship is not control.

Submission is not silence.

Covenant never requires a spouse to endure sin in hiding.

If you are being harmed—physically, sexually, spiritually, or emotionally—**get safe and bring the light.**

Contact emergency services, reach a trusted pastor or elder, or seek qualified help immediately.

God does not command you to stay in the shadows while another's sin devours what He entrusted to you.

These pages imagine repentance, protection, and honor.

Where those are absent, we urge you to step toward safety, truth, and wise care.

Covenant survives in the presence of light—not in secrecy.

A WORD ON COUNSELING, CARE, AND LIMITS

This book is devotional and instructional.

It is **not** professional counseling, psychological treatment, or licensed therapy, nor should it be taken as such.

We reject the modern "therapeutic gospel" that enthrones feelings as final truth.

Yet we also affirm that biblically faithful, trauma-aware clinical care can serve as adjacent help—naming pain while God's Word governs life and repentance governs change.

We write from conviction: what is often called "professional care" is, by its nature, limited—and sometimes distorted—when measured against the truth of God.

This book does not offer therapy.

It offers something deeper:

a covenantal call to obedience under Christ, where real healing and holiness begin.

Instructions

This book is best taken slowly—not as information, but as formation. Each chapter contains four parts:

1. Narrative

A glimpse into real rooms, real marriages, real pressure. Let the stories slow you down and open your heart.

2. Covenant Flame

The core truth of the chapter distilled to its ember—what God is revealing about marriage, order, sacrifice, and love.

3. Strike Points

Concrete actions for husbands, wives, and both together. Not theory. Practice. Steps that change a house.

4. Scripture Strike

A final anchor in God's Word—because truth must outrun feeling.

How to read:

- Take one chapter a day or one a week.

- Read the narrative slowly.

- Pray the Covenant Flame aloud.

- Choose *one* Strike Point and obey it.

- End with the Scripture Strike.

Do not rush.

Covenant is built with small obedience over time.

Preface

A War of Altars

Marriage is not a private comfort.

It is a public witness.

We wrote this book because we have seen covenant at its most fragile—nights where silence had teeth, days when love felt like grit instead of warmth. We have also seen covenant at its most radiant—ordinary couples transformed not by technique, but by obedience to Christ.

This book does not offer illusions of ease.

It calls men to bleed like Christ and women to trust like the Church—not as caricature but as glory.

Our aim is not to give you advice.

It is to give you an altar.

A place to lay down pride, pick up holiness, and rebuild a union that preaches the gospel in the small rooms where no one claps.

If you feel weight as you read, take heart: the cross has weight.

And the God who carries it with you also rebuilds what breaks.

Introduction

Covenant & Fire

Covenant love is not cinematic.

It is not fragile.

It is not shaped by feelings.

It is shaped by a vow stronger than the seasons that test it.

Every marriage tells a story.

Some preach drift.

Some preach comfort.

Some preach survival.

But the marriages that endure—truly endure—are the ones that preach **Christ**.

Not with microphones.

With habits.

With repentance.

With small choices repeated over years until they become a living parable.

This book is the fruit of those parables—our own and those we've stood beside.

It's a field guide for building a marriage that doesn't just make it, but makes Christ visible.

So breathe.

Slow down.

Prepare your heart.

And let the next pages become the steady flame that teaches you how to stand when the wind rises.

Contents

Part I : The Ache

Exposing the Broken Lens

Chapter 1

The Lie We Swallowed

How False Narratives Distort Desire

The rain settled in—steady, unhurried, soft against the windows. Mara stood at the sink, hands still wet, watching the streetlight turn the drops into silver threads. Ethan was home. Somewhere in the house. But they hadn't been home together in months.

They spoke when they had to—school pickups, the tire with the slow leak, what was left in checking. Words that once warmed now crossed the room like strangers: polite, careful, already braced for misunderstanding.

It wasn't anger anymore. Not really. It was quieter—and in its own way, more dangerous: a slow agreement to keep the distance because distance felt safer. Safer than trying. Safer than failing. Safer than hoping.

Mara dried her hands and leaned against the counter. Isn't this supposed to be easier? The old fairy-tale whisper was still alive:

If it's love, it should feel like love. If it hurts this much, maybe you chose wrong.

Another voice slid in behind it—sharper, familiar:

Maybe you're too much. Maybe you're not enough. Don't ask. Don't need. Don't risk.

But a quieter truth pressed in beneath the noise: Covenant isn't measured by warmth. It's measured by what you refuse to drop when warmth thins.

She rehearsed a dozen openings—Hey (too small). We need to talk (too heavy).

She stayed put, bargaining with fear like fear was wisdom.

She knew better. Fear builds walls and calls them safe. Love doesn't grow in safety; it grows in trust. And trust walks into rooms colder than you want and speaks anyway.

Mara stepped into the hallway. The floorboards responded under her weight.

Ethan looked up from the end table where he'd been sorting mail he wasn't reading. His face held what both of them had worn for weeks—caution braided with hope, a truce that looked like peace if you didn't stare too long.

Her chest tightened. This is the moment the fairy tale never showed: no music, no magic words—just a vow tested in silence.

"I don't want the distance anymore," Mara said.

No flourish. No defense. Just a woman tired of invisible walls.

Ethan didn't answer at first. Something uncoiled in his shoulders. A thaw began where frost had lived. He set the mail down slowly, like anything sudden might spook what had just been born.

Marriage isn't failure-avoidance, Mara told the fear. It's faithfulness under fire.

Someone has to die every day—not dramatically, but with restraint, with listening, with the quiet refusal to keep score.

"Me neither," Ethan said.

Barely more than breath. But enough to crack a door in a house that had forgotten how to let light in.

They stood there a moment—not fixing, not explaining—just letting the rain make its soft argument for staying.

Outside was dim and washable. Inside felt newly possible. Fragile, yes. But possible.

Because covenant isn't about never feeling far. It's about refusing to stay there.

Later, when the house was quiet and courage had cooled to calm, the Spirit pressed again—not with accusation but with the clarity that comes when you stop running:

The lie you swallowed wasn't loud. It was comfortable. It promised ease, and ease cannot carry a cross. Shame isn't shepherding you; it's shrinking you. Step toward each other.

In the dark, Mara found Ethan's hand. Simple touch. A beginner's prayer with skin.

Not a solution—just a beginning.

Maybe repentance looks exactly like that: less speech, more staying.

COVENANT FLAME

You were told marriage is a prize for finding the right person.

Covenant says the vow shapes you into the right kind of giver.

You were told sparks prove love.

Covenant says the flame proves itself when you shield it in the wind.

You were told love should be easy.

Covenant says love is holy because it endures what ease cannot carry.

You were told marriage exists to fulfill you.

Covenant says it sanctifies you—for His glory more than your comfort.

Steady fire, not fragile romance.

It steps toward the one you vowed to guard—before the words come easily,

before the fear grows small,

before warmth returns.

STRIKE POINTS

Husband: Where have you chosen distance because it felt safer than risking tenderness—and what small step back toward her can you take today?

Wife: Have you treated your vows as a burden or as a calling—and what fear has kept you from reaching toward him with honesty?

Together: Which lie about marriage shaped your expectations—and how is the Spirit calling you to replace it with covenant truth?

SCRIPTURE STRIKE

"It is better that you should not vow
    than that you should vow and not pay."
    — Ecclesiastes 5:5 (ESV)

CLOSING ECHO

The Mirror

The bathroom light hums. No accusations tonight—only the heavy quiet that weighs more than shouting.

Mara traces her reflection, the faint exhaustion around her eyes, the questions she's carried alone.

"If this isn't what You meant... show me what is."

She doesn't whisper it as an escape.

She whispers it as a turning.

Something shifts—not toward the easy way out, but toward the truth she had been avoiding.

A truth that doesn't rush her... just invites her.

And truth, once welcomed, begins making a home.

Chapter 2

Designed for Covenant

Why We Cannot Thrive Alone

Ethan rolled the ring against his thumb and stepped out into the night. The air was cool—the kind that quiets a whole house without asking permission. Inside, dishes stood like small monuments to the truce they had negotiated.

Tonight's conflict hadn't been dramatic—just a sharpened tone in front of the kids, the "small" kind that stings deeper than it wounds. But the ache below it was older: being unseen in little ways, apologies that paused conflict without healing it, silence that felt safer than truth.

He looked up into the dark.

It pressed the question hard—temptation dressed as logic.

Did I marry the wrong person?

But another voice rose, older than his doubts:

Marriage isn't a human arrangement. It's a divine act. God doesn't make casual covenants.

He could almost hear the pastor from their wedding day, trembling through Matthew 19:6:

"What God has joined together, let no man separate."

He turned the ring again.

I didn't bind myself—God did.

Memory crowded in—Mara's laugh at the altar, his hand shaking as he slid this same ring onto her finger.

Back then forever sounded like tall grass in the wind—wild, light, effortless.

Tonight, it sounded heavier.

Not smaller—just true.

Covenant isn't a subscription, he told himself.

Not conditional.

Not performance based.

Heaven wrote this law.

Difficulty doesn't dissolve vows; it tests them.

What survives isn't my happiness; it's our faithfulness.

He paced the small deck.

He had been faithful with hours, with money, with the thousand errands that keep life moving.

But have I been faithful with posture—faithful in how I carry her heart when mine feels slighted?

It's easier to ask, Did I choose wrong? than to ask, Am I bowing now?

The old protest surfaced:

What if I wasn't following God when I married?

The answer came quiet, sharp:

Immaturity at the altar doesn't void the vow.

It magnifies mercy—and calls you to obedience now.

You don't fix a shaky foundation by tearing down the house.

You submit the house to the Architect.

Reinforce what is weak.

Bow.

Ethan leaned on the rail and let the quiet do its work.

When you said "I do," heaven recorded it.

God's covenants aren't like man's promises—they're sealed in blood, anchored in design, guarded by judgment.

Your union isn't preference-based; it's assigned.

Even hard seasons preach—either something true about God, or something else.

Inside, the house hummed with late-hour sounds: refrigerator, furnace, the soft breathing of children.

He opened the junk drawer looking for nothing—and found their wedding photo.

He stared—not at their faces, but at the space between them.

That invisible thread they once believed in without knowing its weight.

We didn't understand covenant back then.

But we wanted it.

God honors seeds we don't yet know how to water.

The ring caught the light—more than metal.

Evidence in heaven.

Evidence that God had joined him to this woman—to love, protect, forgive; to lead by laying himself down.

The question was no longer Was this right?

It was:

Will I bow now—and make it holy?

He set the photo down.

Not fireworks.

Not certainty.

Just the refusal to keep asking smaller questions.

He rinsed the plates without noise.

Dried his hands.

Walked to the bedroom doorway.

Mara looked up—guarded, but not closed.

"I was wrong tonight," he said, voice steady. "I'm sorry. I'm bowing now—can we start again, tonight?"

Sometimes covenant sounds like apology.

Sometimes it sounds like a man choosing to die first.

Always, it sounds like staying.

He crossed the room and sat on the floor beside the bed, back against the frame like a man taking his post.

No speeches.

Just presence.

The vow, remembered.

Covenant doesn't promise you'll always feel close.

It promises you'll refuse to stay far.

COVENANT FLAME

You were not joined by preference. You were joined by God.

You thought covenant was fragile; it is stronger than your moods.

You thought forever meant ease; covenant makes forever holy.

You do not need a new spouse. You need a bowed heart. Bow now—and make it holy.

STRIKE POINTS

Husband: Are you asking if she was the "right person," or asking if you will be the faithful man?

Wife: Are you leaving room for obedience to grow, or guarding the room against hope?

Together: What would bowing tonight look like in action, not just intention?

SCRIPTURE STRIKE

"Therefore, what God has joined together, let not man separate." — Matthew 19:6

CLOSING ECHO

The Wedding Photo

He slid the picture back into the drawer, not to hide it but to keep it. The house settled deeper into night. He reached for her hand without forcing words, and she let him hold it. Not resolution—promise. The same God who joined them had not left the room.

Chapter 3

Made for One Flame

Recovering the Unity We Were Shaped For

God doesn't make contracts.
He makes covenants.
And you don't get to walk when it gets hard—you get to bleed like Christ.

They sat in the car outside the restaurant, engine ticking as it cooled, rain fogging the glass from the inside. The date had been his idea—a way to repair something frayed. She'd said yes because saying no felt like surrender.

They laughed a little.
Did the small-talk dance.
Then one stray sentence brushed a half-healed place—
and everything seized again.

Now there was only their breathing and the wet hush of tires on the street.

Mara stared through her reflection as if searching for another version of their story. Ethan watched her profile—familiar and far—and felt the ache he rarely confessed:

I don't know how to reach you anymore.

What are we even doing?

A whisper he'd learned to trust rose under the noise:

You weren't joined for comfort. You were joined for covenant.

Old instincts flickered—defend, explain, withdraw.

The quiet had its own gravity; drifting was easier when nothing erupted.

His thumb found the ring he twirled on anxious nights—the one he'd sworn with, the one that still dug into his palm when he clenched his fist.

A contract says, *If you perform, I stay.*

A covenant says, *Even when you fail, I remain.*

He breathed that line like lifeline oxygen.

Across the console, Mara's phone lit up.

A name she hadn't seen in years.

A memory with a pulse.

She let the screen go dark, then tapped it again.

Not going to answer, she told herself.

Just... tired of feeling unseen.

Another truth rose honest and sharp:

Compatibility can't carry covenant.

Sentiment can't shoulder a cross.

If you're waiting for it to feel easier before you stay, she admitted, *you're not married to a person—you're married to a preference.*

She turned the phone face-down, shaken by how quickly her heart reached for an exit.

Ethan caught the movement without knowing the story.

He felt his own pull—toward one more late night at work, toward silence, toward protecting his ego and calling it leadership.

The Spirit pressed:

A cross doesn't speak in clauses.

It bleeds.

You don't rewrite the vow because it hurts.

Hurt is the price; holiness grows from the choosing.

He swallowed.

"I don't know how to fix us," he said, voice small in the steamed dark. "But I won't walk away."

The words weren't poetry.

They were a man choosing where to die.

The old name pulsed again under her palm.

She slid the phone open, hovered, scrolled to the number— and pressed **Delete**.

Not because she felt strong.

Because she had been made for **one flame**.

This isn't cruelty, she told the ache.

This is covenant.

It crucifies pride.

It costs you:

the right to win,

the right to protect your ego,

the right to withdraw,

the right to walk when it's hard.

Outside, a server dragged metal chairs across wet concrete.

Inside, Mara reached across the console—not ready for a speech, ready for a small obedience. Ethan took her hand like a man grabbing rope in a current.

Leaving isn't escape, he told his fear.
It's violation.
God's covenant love never says, "I'm done with you."
Neither should mine.

They sat like that for a long time—two sinners under one vow, letting the rain do the talking, choosing to bleed where they once bargained.

The heater clicked on.

The windows cleared.

Not resolution.

Alignment.

COVENANT FLAME

You were not made for many fires.
You were joined to **one holy flame**.
   Guard it.
Feed it.
Die to keep it burning.

STRIKE POINTS

Husband:

Where are you choosing comfort over crucifixion?

Name **one exit** you've been taking—emotional, mental, or habitual—and close it today.

Wife:

What "safer" attention, memory, or imagined rescue have you kept on reserve?

Delete it. Bring the ache into the light.

Together:

What practice this week will feed your one flame—prayer aloud, confession, a guarded boundary, or choosing presence when emotions lag?

SCRIPTURE STRIKE

"Set me as a seal upon your heart,
as a seal upon your arm,
for love is strong as death...
Many waters cannot quench love,
neither can floods drown it."
— *Song of Solomon 8:6–7*

CLOSING ECHO

The Number

Back home, the house exhaled in familiar creaks. She stood in the hallway's thin light and opened her phone one more time—not to look for the name, but to make sure it was gone. It was.

He came up behind her, not crowding, just present. No speeches.

He reached past her to turn off the lamp, then waited.

Her hand found his in the dark.

Warmth, small as a candle, held.

The flame didn't roar.
It refused to die.

Part II – The Weight

Headship & Submission in Their True Form

Chapter 4

Headship Is Sacrifice

Carrying the Cross, Not the Crown

Y ou are the head. That means you die first—
not in glory,
but in quiet,
in frustration,
and sometimes in blood.

Mara was crying in the hallway. He didn't know why. Dinner had been ordinary—dishes, homework, bedtime. Nothing sharp. Nothing explosive. She'd been quiet, but not angry. Now her arms were crossed, eyes red, her whole body braced like a door against weather.

"You never fight for me," she whispered. "You just... move on. Like I'm not even here."

The old shame rose fast—the boyhood ache that he wasn't enough, that effort never counted, that whatever he gave would still be judged lacking. Instinct said shut down. Let the garage swallow him and call it peace.

He didn't.

He stepped forward—not with speeches, just presence. Six feet felt like a canyon. He crossed it anyway. A Lego under his heel, the hum of the fridge, her breath hitching once—ordinary sounds inside a holy moment.

Something in you dies here, the Spirit pressed. *Go first.*

You are the head, he reminded his pride. That does not mean you win. It means you go first—into surrender, into humility, into death. If you demand her submission while refusing sacrifice, you're not leading—you're hiding.

He reached for her hand. It didn't melt the moment, but it kept the moment from hardening. No tone charts. No relitigating bedtime logistics. Say the truer thing.

"I didn't fight for you, Mara. I'm sorry."

When Eden shattered, God's question wasn't to both; it was to Adam: *"Where are you?"* (Genesis 3:9)

If this house is cold, He asks **me** first.

If she's bitter, He asks **me** first.

If the kids are afraid, He asks **me** first.

Not because the man causes everything—but because head means he answers first.

He felt tired. He'd been tired for months. Tired is real—but it is not an alibi. He slid his phone across the counter, screen down—like setting down a sword he'd been pointing the wrong way. He stayed. Long enough for tears to become sentences. Long enough for the edge to leave her voice.

This is the work:

Absorb the insult; answer with grace.

Take her silence; answer with presence.

Lose the argument; win the war by serving.

Hold the line when nobody claps.

Christ died while we were still enemies.

You die while she's still cold.

You die before she comes back.

You die with no guarantee she will.

His mind flicked through ledgers—where he'd kept score, punished with distance, waited for her to go first so he could feel justified going second.

I used headship as a hedge, he realized. *It covered my comfort, not her heart.*

Weak men blame. Holy men bleed.

You don't get to say, *"Well, she doesn't respect me."*

You don't get to say, *"She's not doing her part."*

You don't get to say, *"I'm exhausted."* You are exhausted. That's part of the call.

She doesn't need your power; she needs your posture—a man bowed before God, not towering to feel in control.

He wanted a timeline. A technique. Something a podcast could package. But obedience isn't a therapy schedule. *Don't wait to feel ready,* he told himself. *Obey now, even while it hurts.* Counseling can name pain; truth must confront rebellion. If you delay obedience until your feelings agree, you're not healing—you're negotiating.

He took a breath.

"What would make you feel fought for tonight, Mara?"

Not someday. **Tonight.**

"Stay with me," she said. "Don't retreat. Pray with me before we sleep."

It felt small. It felt holy.

Later, the house fell quiet. He walked the hallway, pausing at each child's door like posting angels with whispered prayers. In the garage he stood a long time, engine off, lights out. The silence wasn't a hiding place anymore—it was an altar.

"Where I've used headship to protect me, God, forgive me," he said into the dark. "If something must die here, let it be my pride."

He went back inside.

Headship isn't license; it's crucifixion—for her good.

You are not owed respect.

You are assigned a cross.

And the weight of your house will either crush you in pride—

or be lifted by your obedience to die first.

COVENANT FLAME

You weren't chosen to be served.

You were called to be spent.

Headship is not a throne to occupy;

it is a cross to carry—

first, longest, and most unseen.

A husband leads by being the first to die

to pride,

to retreat,

to coldness,

to defensiveness.

The house is shaped by the man who bleeds for it—

not once,

but daily.

STRIKE POINTS

Husband: Where have you been waiting for her to soften before you lead? Name the place you must bow tonight—and bow.

Wife: Are you watching for genuine death of his pride, or punishing him for how slowly it dies?

Together: Does the man in your home lead by demand—or by dying? What would sacrificial leadership look like this week?

SCRIPTURE STRIKE

"Husbands, love your wives, as Christ loved the church and gave himself up for her." — *Ephesians 5:25*

CLOSING ECHO

The Garage

He sat in the dim, engine off, nothing humming but his breath.

The fight hadn't been loud, but it had been true.

She had asked for presence, not perfection.

He had hidden behind fatigue, not the cross.

Tonight, the truth finally found him.

"This is what I've done with my headship," he admitted into the quiet.

"I used it to protect me—not her."

No dramatic music.

No instant change.

Just a vow forming in the dark—

a man deciding what must die

so his house can live.

He turned off the light and went inside.You are the head. That means you die first—

not in glory,

but in quiet,

in frustration,

and sometimes in blood.

Mara was crying in the hallway. He didn't know why. Dinner had been ordinary—dishes, homework, bedtime. Nothing sharp. Nothing explosive. She'd been quiet, but not angry. Now her arms were crossed, eyes red, her whole body braced like a door against weather.

"You never fight for me," she whispered. "You just... move on. Like I'm not even here."

The old shame rose fast—the boyhood ache that he wasn't enough, that effort never counted, that whatever he gave would still be judged lacking. Instinct said shut down. Let the garage swallow him and call it peace.

He didn't.

He stepped forward—not with speeches, just presence. Six feet felt like a canyon. He crossed it anyway. A Lego under his heel, the hum of the fridge, her breath hitching once—ordinary sounds inside a holy moment.

Something in you dies here, the Spirit pressed. *Go first.*

You are the head, he reminded his pride. That does not mean you win. It means you go first—into surrender, into humility, into death. If you demand her submission while refusing sacrifice, you're not leading—you're hiding.

He reached for her hand. It didn't melt the moment, but it kept the moment from hardening. No tone charts. No relitigating bedtime logistics. Say the truer thing.

"I didn't fight for you, Mara. I'm sorry."

When Eden shattered, God's question wasn't to both; it was to Adam: *"Where are you?"* (Genesis 3:9)

If this house is cold, He asks **me** first.

If she's bitter, He asks **me** first.

If the kids are afraid, He asks **me** first.

Not because the man causes everything—but because head means he answers first.

He felt tired. He'd been tired for months. Tired is real—but it is not an alibi. He slid his phone across the counter, screen down—like setting down a sword he'd been pointing the wrong way. He stayed. Long enough for tears to become sentences. Long enough for the edge to leave her voice.

This is the work:

Absorb the insult; answer with grace.

Take her silence; answer with presence.

Lose the argument; win the war by serving.

Hold the line when nobody claps.

Christ died while we were still enemies.

You die while she's still cold.

You die before she comes back.

You die with no guarantee she will.

His mind flicked through ledgers—where he'd kept score, punished with distance, waited for her to go first so he could feel justified going second.

I used headship as a hedge, he realized. *It covered my comfort, not her heart.*

Weak men blame. Holy men bleed.

You don't get to say, *"Well, she doesn't respect me."*

You don't get to say, *"She's not doing her part."*

You don't get to say, *"I'm exhausted."* You are exhausted. That's part of the call.

She doesn't need your power; she needs your posture—a man bowed before God, not towering to feel in control.

He wanted a timeline. A technique. Something a podcast could package. But obedience isn't a therapy schedule. *Don't wait to feel ready,* he told himself. *Obey now, even while it hurts.* Counseling can name pain; truth must confront rebellion. If you delay obedience until your feelings agree, you're not healing—you're negotiating.

He took a breath.

"What would make you feel fought for tonight, Mara?"

Not someday. **Tonight.**

"Stay with me," she said. "Don't retreat. Pray with me before we sleep."

It felt small. It felt holy.

Later, the house fell quiet. He walked the hallway, pausing at each child's door like posting angels with whispered prayers. In the garage he stood a long time, engine off, lights out. The silence wasn't a hiding place anymore—it was an altar.

"Where I've used headship to protect me, God, forgive me," he said into the dark. "If something must die here, let it be my pride."

He went back inside.

Headship isn't license; it's crucifixion—for her good.

You are not owed respect.

You are assigned a cross.

And the weight of your house will either crush you in pride—

or be lifted by your obedience to die first.

COVENANT FLAME

You weren't chosen to be served.

You were called to be spent.

Headship is not a throne to occupy;

it is a cross to carry—

first, longest, and most unseen.

A husband leads by being the first to die

to pride,

to retreat,

to coldness,

to defensiveness.

The house is shaped by the man who bleeds for it—

not once,

but daily.

STRIKE POINTS

Husband: Where have you been waiting for her to soften before you lead? Name the place you must bow tonight—and bow.

Wife: Are you watching for genuine death of his pride, or punishing him for how slowly it dies?

Together: Does the man in your home lead by demand—or by dying? What would sacrificial leadership look like this week?

SCRIPTURE STRIKE

"Husbands, love your wives, as Christ loved the church and gave himself up for her." — *Ephesians 5:25*

CLOSING ECHO

The Garage

He sat in the dim, engine off, nothing humming but his breath.
The fight hadn't been loud, but it had been true.
She had asked for presence, not perfection.
He had hidden behind fatigue, not the cross.
Tonight, the truth finally found him.

"This is what I've done with my headship," he admitted into the quiet.
"I used it to protect me—not her."

No dramatic music.
No instant change.
Just a vow forming in the dark—
a man deciding what must die
so his house can live.

He turned off the light and went inside.

Chapter 5

Submission Is Strength

The Hidden Power of Yielding

S he was never meant to carry the weight of headship. But when she reflects the Church, she reflects glory.

Mara stood at the sink, hands in the water, heat fogging the window while the house pulsed around her—kids running, dinner half-made, laundry like a tide that never recedes. Ethan was home, technically. Present in body, absent in spirit. The ache rose the way it always did: that thin, tired question—Why do I have to hold everything together? She swallowed it. Not to disappear—to bring it somewhere holy.

"God... how do I honor You in this?" she whispered—half confession, half plea.

Submission isn't erasure, she reminded the old fear. It isn't fear. It isn't permission to be walked on. It's strength under God—ordered power, not a muted presence. It's a heart that knows where the throne actually is.

She dried her hands and leaned on the counter, listening to the room settle. She remembered the early days—the bright vows, his laughter in the hall. She also remembered the drift: decisions made without her, little closures that taught her to be quiet. Once, quiet felt like safety. Now it felt like a room without air.

The Church isn't mute before Christ, she thought. She sings. She weeps. She intercedes. She speaks—under covering, for life.

A wife reflects the Church. Which means she reflects joyful obedience, steady trust, fierce intercession—surrender that flows from identity, not from fear.

She picked up the dishtowel and set it down again. Waiting doesn't have to be weakness. Silence doesn't have to be despair. When I wait on God, I'm choosing not to swing. My voice isn't gone; it's timed.

A verse she'd tucked away surfaced: "...the woman is the glory of man." (1 Cor. 11:7) Glory doesn't mean lesser, she told her shame. Glory means magnified—strength made visible, beauty reflected.

She thought of last night—another plan made without her. It stung like being written out of her own story. She had wanted to prove, press, push. Instead, she'd prayed in the pantry until heat in her chest turned to tears. By the time she came out, the moment for truth had passed. Tonight I'll try again, she decided—without the edge, without the need to win.

Bow to God, not to sin, the Spirit pressed. Bow to design, not to domination. Bow because God is perfect—not because your husband is.

So she would not rebel when he was flawed. She would not seize control when he was passive. She would not compete when she could simply be faithful. She would pray. She would wait. She would speak—in season, with weight.

Submission isn't silence; it's timing. Not absence of voice; alignment of voice.

She rinsed the last plate, turned off the water, and breathed. She could feel the old current—anger dressed as courage, independence dressed as strength. It always promised relief. It never delivered peace.

Rebellion feels righteous at first, she admitted. It tastes like oxygen to a starving heart. But it ends in exposure, not covering.

A woman out from under covering may feel free, she thought. But exposed isn't empowered. Exposed is endangered.

Covering is not a cage. Headship that bleeds is a refuge, not a prison. Under that kind of love, submission becomes a crown.

She wiped the counter, gathered the socks, and let the ache turn into intercession. Not for a different life—for this life to be threaded with glory again. If he won't pray yet, I will, she thought. Not as the head—never that—but as a watchtower no one sees.

Intercession isn't a consolation prize. It's a weapon. When I pray in secret, hell loses ground it thought it owned.

She glanced toward the living room—he was there, scrolling, distant. She didn't need to perform strength for him. She needed to host God in this house. The room felt different already—not because circumstances shifted, but because her posture did.

Obedience before God precedes fruit with man. Honor clears a channel where correction can land. Submission gives truth its music.

Tonight I'll speak—briefly, clearly, without the courtroom tone, she told herself. And if timing isn't right, I'll wait again. Not for approval. For God.

Submission is not weakness. It is glory, yielded. It is the Church magnifying Christ—not by leading Him, but by trusting Him.

COVENANT FLAME

You do not reflect weakness —
you reflect **glory, yielded**.
The Church does not lead Christ;
she magnifies Him.

    Your power is not in force,
but in fragrance —
the kind that fills a house and steadies it again.

    Submission never tolerates sin or abuse;
it stands **under God**,
speaks in season,
waits in strength,
and shines with a beauty that covering protects,
not diminishes.

STRIKE POINTS

Wife: Are you submitting *to God through your husband* —
or reacting *to your husband instead of God*?
Choose one sentence of **timed truth** you will bring this week.

    Husband: Are you welcoming her wisdom and intercession,
or guarding your ego by shrinking her voice?
Name one way you will **invite and honor** her counsel.

    Together: Does your home sound like the Church —
reverent, truthful, at peace —
or like culture: defensive, loud, afraid?
Pick one rhythm (prayer aloud, screens sleeping in the kitchen, weekly

check-in)

to restore **tone.**

SCRIPTURE STRIKE

"Wives, submit to your own husbands, as to the Lord...

as the church submits to Christ,

so also wives should submit in everything to their husbands."

— *Ephesians 5:22, 24*

CLOSING ECHO

The Stairwell

She sat halfway up the stairs — not at the top, not at the bottom —

the quiet middle where decisions gather weight.

He was in the living room; they hadn't spoken in an hour.

The old self would have pushed, pressed, proven.

Tonight she let the sermon be her posture.

This time, silence is strength.

This time, waiting is war.

She wasn't giving up.

She was handing the outcome back to God.

In the surrender, something unclenched — not powerlessness, but peace.

Submission had never meant disappearing.

It had always meant **trust.**

And in trust, glory began to glow again —
low at first, then steady —
lighting the way back down the stairs.

Chapter 6

Marriage Is Warfare

Standing Shoulder to Shoulder Against Darkness

Y our marriage is not just emotional. It is spiritual. And the battle isn't just between you—it's against what you were made to reflect.

They'd been good for weeks. Praying again. Laughing again. Even the awkward places had softened.

Then one look—one word—one tiny miss—and the floor gave way. Her stomach dropped. His jaw set.

The fork clinked too hard in the sink. Heat rose in the room like a stovetop left on.

"Really?" she said—too fast.

Ethan stared at the counter, not at her. "Forget it."

Silence fell—the kind that hums.

Mara stood at the sink, palms in suds gone cold. Her hands shook once; she hid it under the water, staring at the single glass he'd left like it was a message. Ethan sat in the car with the door half-shut, keys in his hand, breathing like a man who'd outrun something and wasn't sure what.

Why now—when we were okay? she thought, wiping the same circle on the counter three times. The whisper came back—quiet, steady: War doesn't wait for peace. It attacks what threatens its kingdom.

Ethan pressed his forehead to the steering wheel. The old shame hissed, You always mess this up. He answered it out loud: "No." Covenant preaches even when we're bad at it—Christ and His Church, without a microphone. If hell can't break it, it will try to dull it. He could feel the old weapons within reach: withdrawal, winning the argument in his head, being "above" it.

He went back inside. She didn't move. The clock in the hall ticked loud as a metronome for pride.

"I'm not your enemy," he said—too rough, but true.

She blinked hard. Then stop acting like it wanted to come out. Instead she swallowed and tried again. "I don't want to fight you," she said. "I want to fight what keeps taking our peace."

They sat at the table, chairs turned a little toward each other, not across. Hands on wood. Shoulders high. The air smelled like lemon soap and something tense.

"Okay," he said, softer. "Name what you felt—not what I am."

"I felt invisible," she said, eyes on a knot in the table. "Like the glass was a list of what I carry alone."

He nodded once. "I felt judged before I could breathe." The words cost him. He exhaled. "I'm sorry."

Her fingers tapped the table—once, twice—then she reached across. Their hands met like truce flags.

We do not wrestle against flesh and blood... drifted up from somewhere deep (Eph. 6:12).

My spouse isn't my target, he reminded himself. The accuser is.

"Can we pray?" she asked. "I don't have a speech."

They inhaled like swimmers before a dive and bowed. Not pretty. Real.

"Jesus," he said, "we're on the same side. We forgot."

"Teach us to bless," she whispered, "when cursing would feel better."

"Close our mouths when the enemy baits us."

"Open them to confess fast."

"Guard this table."

Something eased. Not solved—eased. Like a window cracked after a long winter.

They took small ground with small choices.

"I'm sorry for the tone," he said.

"I forgive you," she answered, wincing at how hard that always is to say first.

She stood and rinsed the glass. He dried it without being asked. The normal sound of a dish towel on ceramic felt like the line moved forward one inch.

Every pride that bent felt like a sword swing. Every forgiveness that landed felt like air returning to a stuffy room. Every "let's pray" when they would rather prosecute pushed the dark back—one wall, one lie, one evening.

He looked at her—the real her, eyes a little red, brave anyway. She looked at him—tired, imperfect, still hers. The room changed temperature. No applause. Just presence.

"Same team," he said, and meant it.

"Same King," she answered.

They ate the rest of dinner cold—and together. His knee touched hers under the table and didn't move.

COVENANT FLAME

You are not merely married —
you are **armed**,
assigned,
and **watched by heaven**.
   Hell attacks covenant because covenant preaches Christ.
So guard your tone, your unity, your table.
   Every confession is a sword.
Every forgiveness is ground reclaimed.
Every "same team" pushes darkness back an inch at a time.
   Bow before God.
Stand beside each other.
Speak life in rooms that smell like smoke.

STRIKE POINTS

Husband:
Where are you passive in the war?
Pick up one weapon today:
- pray aloud
- confess first
- take gentle initiative
Choose the one you least want to choose.
   Wife:
Are you fighting *him* —
or fighting *for* him?

Choose one intercession to speak over his name
every day this week.
Together:
Pick one place to pray for 14 days straight
(front door, dinner table, bedside).
Don't wait for calm.
Make it.

SCRIPTURE STRIKE

"For we do not wrestle against flesh and blood,
but against the rulers...
against the spiritual forces of evil in the heavenly places."
— *Ephesians 6:12*

CLOSING ECHO

The Front Door

He checked the deadbolt, clicked off the porch light.
She closed the dishwasher and wiped the last ring of water from the
counter.
  In bed, their hands found each other under the covers —
not dramatic, not triumphant,
just faithful.
  "We're tired," he said — confession, not excuse.
"We're still on the same side," she answered.

Two hands.
One King.
War — met with covenant.

Chapter 7

Submission Is Not Silence

The Courage to Speak in Honor

S ubmission is not erasure. It is ordered strength. Holy strength. And it speaks—not to control, but to cover.

Ethan made another decision without her. Small on paper, huge in the heart. The ache tightened under Mara's ribs, the way air does when you've been holding your breath too long. It wasn't that she wanted to run the house. She wanted to be in it with him—heart and mind.

She wasn't angry so much as heartsore. I don't want to rebel, she thought. I want to be seen.

Mara dried her hands, pressed her palms to the counter, and prayed the sentence that has rescued more marriages than speeches ever have: God... teach me how to speak under You.

Submission isn't silence, she reminded the old fear. It's Spirit-led speech under covering. Strength that refuses to disappear. I won't numb my voice to survive. I won't bury discernment to keep a fake peace. I'll give truth a tone that honors You.

She found Ethan in the living room—half-turned toward a screen, half-turned away from her. Mara sat—not as a judge, but as a woman who belongs. Her hands trembled; she breathed until the tremor became clarity.

"When decisions are made without me," Mara said gently, "I feel small in a story I'm supposed to live with you. I want to stand beside you, not trail behind your plans."

Ethan opened his mouth to defend—then closed it. He heard the tremor, the ache, the restraint. He also heard the honor. It disarmed him more than anger ever had.

Headship sets the lead, he told himself. Love makes room. Leadership isn't solitary; it's hospitable. Invite her counsel. Die to the ego when she brings hard truth with grace. Her voice isn't a threat to your headship; it mirrors your stewardship.

"When I don't loop you in, what happens to you?" Ethan asked, elbows on his knees.

"I start managing my hurt by taking control," Mara said, eyes low. "It makes me strong for a minute and exhausted for a week. I don't want that kind of strength. I want holy strength."

Ethan nodded, slower now—like a man setting a weapon down. "I was wrong. I made it easier on me and expensive for you." He exhaled. "I want your voice. I need it."

Mara didn't take a throne. She took his hand.

When a woman isn't heard in her own home, she doesn't always shout, Mara thought. Sometimes she goes numb. Sometimes she walks away in her heart. And when she stops speaking, the marriage stops breathing.

"You're not my adversary," Ethan said. "You're my ally."

"Then ask me in," Mara answered. "Before the choice is made. Not for a rubber stamp—so we can see it whole."

Honor felt like oxygen. The room drew a deeper breath.

They talked details—short, simple. A date on the calendar. Who calls whom. What "asking in" sounds like. No courtroom tone. No retreat. Just a husband opening space and a wife filling it with wisdom instead of withdrawal.

Silence is not submission. Loudness is not rebellion. True submission is vocal, wise, patient, holy. And a godly man blesses that voice—he doesn't punish it.

COVENANT FLAME

Submission is not disappearing —
it is **belonging under God**.

A wife's voice, given in honor,
is not competition —
it is **covering**.

A husband's headship, given in love,
is not control —
it is **making room for breath**.

When honor shapes tone and truth shapes timing,
marriage becomes the place where both can speak without fear.

STRIKE POINTS

Wife:

Have you gone quiet just to survive —

or are you speaking with Spirit-led clarity and trust?
Write *one sentence of truth in honor*
and bring it this week.

   Husband:
Do you bless her voice —
or merely tolerate it until she falls silent?
Name one decision you will invite her into
before it is made.

   Together:
Does your home sound like the Church —
reverent, truthful, slow to anger —
or like a courtroom?
Choose tone first.
Then talk.

SCRIPTURE STRIKE

"The heart of her husband trusts in her...
She opens her mouth with wisdom,
and the teaching of kindness is on her tongue."
— *Proverbs 31:11, 26*

CLOSING ECHO

The Table

Later they sat across from each other with two mugs and no defenses.
She didn't posture.
He didn't retreat.

He reached for her hand,
held it like a vow,
and looked her in the eyes.

"I see you," he said.
"I'm sorry I made you feel small.
I want your voice.
I need it."

She didn't cry,
but something loosened in her chest.

The room drew a deeper breath —
not because he surrendered control,
but because he made space.

And in that space,
trust began to sound like worship again.

Chapter 8

Train Your Replacement

Building Beyond Your Own Lifetime

Y ou are not the hero of your home. Christ is. You're here to pass the flame, not carry it alone.

The house was quiet after dinner, plates stacked but not yet washed. Ethan sat at the table with his Bible open, prayer still hanging in the air like warmth. From the hallway came a shuffle of bare feet. His son stopped in the doorway—hair up like a question mark, eyes wide but not asking.

No words. Just watching. Watching the way Ethan turned the pages. Watching the same hands that had steadied Mara's shoulder in the kitchen. Watching how he carried hard days without handing out blame.

He didn't come for a lecture, Ethan realized. He came for a flame.

Ethan lifted a hand—no speech, just welcome—and the boy crossed the threshold, climbed into the chair, and leaned against his arm. Not because he understood. Because he knew where the fire lived.

Our vow was never meant to be a private comfort, Ethan thought. It's a light others can see.

Marriage isn't performance; it's pattern. Every tone he took. Every sigh he let slip. Every way he held Mara on an ordinary Tuesday—it all built something in the ones watching. This vow doesn't stop at the altar; it either spreads or it withers.

He winced at memories of doing everything alone and calling it love: pay the bills, fix the hinge, absorb the stress, keep Mara free from worry. Noble, maybe—but over time she had grown quiet, her strength muffled by the walls he thought were protection.

Protection without participation isn't covering, the Spirit pressed. It looks like care, but it locks her out.

God hadn't given Ethan a helper to rubber-stamp his certainty. He'd given him a mirror, a discerner, a shield-bearer. If I don't train her hand, the house stands half-covered in the war.

Invite her wisdom, he told himself. Build with her—not just for her. Headship makes room, or it isn't headship at all.

Down the hallway their daughter laughed—high and unguarded. Ethan felt the future in it—and the weight.

Children aren't waiting for a sermon, he thought. They're being discipled by our patterns. They absorb what we normalize. They inherit what we tolerate.

A boy becomes a man long before he learns a definition. He learns by watching in small rooms: how you touch Mara with kindness, how you repent without a press release, how you carry silence without weaponizing it, how you pray when no one claps.

A girl learns the shape of safety from the way her mother is treated. If honor lives in your house, it will live in her bones. If blame rules, fear will too.

We're not raising behavior, he reminded his tired heart. We're raising witnesses. One day they will either carry this flame—or run from the fire we made of it.

Ethan closed the Bible and slid it an inch toward his son. Not pushing. Inviting. Later, he would hand the budget to Mara—not as homework, but as partnership. Later, he would let his son stumble through the bedtime prayer; let his daughter bless the meal with a voice still shaky. Later, he would ask Mara to lead a psalm so the house could hear the strength God had placed in her.

You're not building a stage, he told himself. You're building a home that can burn without you.

Build with Mara. Bless her strength. Let the children hear the sound of surrender, not just control.

Obedience is the legacy. The fire belongs to God. You only pass it forward.

COVENANT FLAME

Covenant is not performance —
it is **preparation**.

A holy man does not build dependence;
he builds **disciples**.

He does not guard the flame to feel needed;
he gives it away so they can stand when he no longer can.

Legacy is not what you leave behind —
it's what you **train into the ones watching now**.

STRIKE POINTS

Husband:
Are you making space for your wife to build with you —
or doing everything yourself to feel necessary?
Name one area where you will **hand her the plans**
instead of carrying them alone.

Wife:
Are you ready to carry fire with him —
or waiting to be carried?
Choose one place to lead this week:
a prayer, a psalm, a plan, a blessing.

Together:
What will your children absorb this week —
honor or hurry, repentance or spin,
shared prayer or shared silence?
Pick one pattern to model **on purpose**,
even if no one claps.

SCRIPTURE STRIKE

"What you have heard from me in the presence of many witnesses,
entrust to faithful men
who will be able to teach others also."
— *2 Timothy 2:2*

CLOSING ECHO

The Firekeeper's Son

He didn't ask questions —
just set his small hand on the open page beside his father's
and bowed his head.
    Ethan didn't preach or explain.
He slid the Bible a little closer
and prayed again —
two voices, one flame.
    From the doorway Mara watched,
then stepped forward and placed a hand on each shoulder.
    Their shadows stretched across the wall —
not performance,
but a vow alive in the next generation,
the fire already passing forward.

Part III – The Fire

Testing the Bond Under Pressure

Chapter 9

The War Against Order

Why the Enemy Hates Covenant

D isorder isn't neutral. It's an attack. The war for your marriage begins with what you permit.

Eve didn't mean to stand that close to the tree. The air itself seemed to hold its breath. She knew the boundary. She trusted the One who walked with them when the day cooled. Still, a voice found a seam.

"Did God really say?"

Not through Adam. Around him.

It wasn't her weakness the serpent hunted. It was the pattern. If order could bend, the bond would fray. Her fingers hovered over the fruit, but his voice stayed in his chest. She took. She ate. He watched. And something in the world slipped out of joint with a quiet sound no one forgets.

It was never about the fruit. It was about structure—who would speak, who would cover, who would stand.

From that hour the enemy learned a simple door: invert the order, and invasion follows.

Years later—another house, another night—the same door waited in a hallway where a lamp hummed and a sink held two dishes that felt heavier than they looked. Mara had carried the bedtime prayer three nights now. Carried the budget with the red line. Carried the hard talk with their son who hid pain under jokes. None of it was a speech. Just the slow weight you lift because it will crush someone if you don't.

Ethan loved her. He loved their children. He wasn't cruel. He was careful. He told himself that silence might turn into peace if he gave it room.

Inversion rarely starts as rebellion. It starts as delay. Delay learns to call itself wisdom—and that "wisdom" forgets how to speak.

Mara stood with one hand on the back of a chair. Ethan set his phone face-down and rubbed the bridge of his nose. The refrigerator ticked. The floor creaked. The house was full of small noises and one large silence.

Marriage was meant to preach before it pleased, she remembered. Christ covers and gives Himself; the Church trusts and follows. Disorder isn't about preferences—it's stepping outside God's design. Ignore that, and the enemy walks in through the door you left open.

When the pattern flips, you see it in small rooms. Wives become the spiritual initiators while husbands drift the edges, comfortable in the absence of conflict, calling it peace. Headship becomes a punchline in the world. Submission becomes a slur. "Equality" turns into a velvet word that erases the image you were made to mirror.

What's lost isn't only roles. It's glory. The parable goes quiet. The Bride doesn't lead her Lord. Equal in worth. Distinct in role. Holy in order.

Ethan looked up and found Mara's eyes. No accusation there—just a question that felt like a hand held out over a narrow stream: Will you cross? Will you stand?

Headship isn't noise, he told his fear. Submission isn't disappearance. Order is love with a spine.

He let the shame rise and pass. Let the fear of failing again settle like silt. Then he spoke. Not loud. Steady.

"Let's gather the children. It's bedtime."

They walked the hall together. Doors opened. Socks whispered on carpet. They formed a circle on the rug where the pile was thinnest. He didn't perform. He named what God had said, where they had let it bend, and what would be different now. She didn't shrink. She answered with strength at his side. Their son's jaw loosened. Their daughter's shoulder lowered against her mother. The room felt like a window had opened somewhere you couldn't see.

When he speaks first, the weight settles.

When she answers, the room exhales.

Prayer rose without polish and landed with weight. Not magic. Just the roof fastening back down. The wind would have to work harder to get in.

Later, the dishes were stacked. The lamp ticked as it cooled. They stood in the doorway to their children's room and listened to the soft breath of sleep.

"Thank you," she said.

"For what?" He truly didn't know which part she meant.

"For not leaving me to carry a place I wasn't made to carry alone."

He nodded, and the nod felt like repentance with skin on it. She touched his sleeve. The quiet this time didn't feel like avoidance. It felt like shelter.

You don't fix everything in a night. You choose where you will stand, and the house learns your shape again. You choose again tomorrow. And the next day. And the whisper finds fewer seams.

COVENANT FLAME

Don't trade God's pattern
for a ceasefire with the serpent.
Let the man **bear**.
Let the woman **breathe**.
Order is not outdated —
it is **holy**.
When a home stands in alignment under Christ,
the enemy loses his doorway.
Disorder doesn't creep in by force —
it walks through whatever door we leave ajar.

STRIKE POINTS

Husband:
Where have you been calling silence **"peace"**?
Name one place you will **speak and stand** tonight.
Wife:
What weight have you carried faithfully
that you can now set down under covering?
Name it — and hand it over.
Together:
Which corner of your home has drifted out of order?

Restore it before you sleep:
name it, pray it, act.

SCRIPTURE STRIKE

"The head of every man is Christ,
the head of a wife is her husband,
and the head of Christ is God."
— *1 Corinthians 11:3*

CLOSING ECHO

The Door Ajar

They left the door open on purpose.
A thin strip of light lay across the hallway
like a quiet vow.

   Two shadows leaned together on the wall —
his a little broader,
hers a little nearer —
neither one swallowing the other.

   In the next room,
the slow breath of children at rest.
The serpent still whispers,
but there is no soft place to land.

   The house has a spine again.
And the light keeps watch.

Chapter 10

Headship Is Not a Weapon

Guarding Against Abuse of Authority

Small group night. Shoes by the door. A pot of chili. A living room that felt safe most weeks.

They were sharing "what's next"—work shifts changing, a teen learning to drive, a couple starting foster classes. Mara hesitated, then said it: she'd been looking at a few things—serving at the weeknight shelter, a two-day retreat she'd circled twice, maybe launching a tiny side project from the kitchen. Nothing dramatic. Just movement.

Ethan smiled, easy. "Good ideas," he said. "Just... probably not this season. Things are tight. We should be realistic."

It sounded sensible. It always did.

Mara folded her hands. "I've brought these up for a year," she said quietly. "It's never no. It's just never yes. My words don't move anything."

Silence settled in the room—not a courtroom silence; a caring one.

Ethan felt the old defense rise: budgets, the calendar, stability. "I'm not shutting you down," he said, trying to sound reasonable. "I'm just... protecting us."

The study leader cleared his throat. "Can I open Scripture for a minute?" He didn't reach for a verse to end a debate. He turned to Ephesians 5 and read slowly: "Husbands, love your wives, as Christ loved the church and gave himself up for her."

He looked up. "Help me understand," he said to Ethan, voice gentle. "In the last year, what did it cost you to help Mara move forward? Not what it would cost. What it actually did cost."

Ethan opened his mouth, but nothing came out.

The leader tried again. "If Jesus gives Himself up for His Bride, what would giving-yourself-up look like here? In time, in money, in inconvenience?"

Ethan felt heat rise under his collar. "We have kids. Work. It's complicated."

A friend across the room nodded slowly. "I get the instinct," he said. "I called it wisdom too. It was fear. My wife didn't need my reasons. She needed my actions to shift so her 'yes' actually moved something."

The room stayed quiet. The slow cooker clicked.

Ethan looked at Mara—the careful way she was breathing like a swimmer saving air. He didn't repent on the spot. He just said, "I need to sit with this," and he meant it.

They drove home mostly silent. In the driveway he kept his hands on the wheel after the engine stopped. He remembered their daughter at the sink last week, saying it like a fact: "Mom has ideas, but Dad decides what's best for the family." He remembered the retreat brochure on the fridge that had turned into a coaster for magnets and jokes.

Sleep didn't come easy.

By lunch the next day, the sentences had sharpened. Not dramatic—honest. I say "not now" because it costs me nothing, he admitted. I call it "realistic" because it keeps me comfortable. That's not Jesus. He texted his brother: I minimize Mara and call it wisdom. Can I call you tonight? Then he made a list of every "maybe later" from the last year. The column was longer than he wanted.

After work he didn't make a speech. He asked her to sit at the table. He put the list down between them.

"I've called it 'realistic,'" he said, finally steady. "But it's been fear and control. I've kept saying 'not now' because it was easier on me. I'm sorry. Not in general—these specifically." He tapped the list. "That's not Jesus."

She didn't rush to smooth it over. "Thank you," she said. "I need to know my voice matters—that it can move something."

"Then let's move it," he answered. "You pick one. I will make it work."

They built it small and real:

Two-voice rule: No ongoing "maybe later." If he says "not now," he brings a dated plan with a first step and what he will do to make it happen.

Budget line for her calling: set and funded (retreat deposit, shelter commute, starter supplies).

Calendar block: his initials on kid-duty during her commitments—ink, not pencil.

Weekly check-in: two men would text him Fridays, "What did you do to move Mara forward?" One woman would check with her, "Are you getting the support you need to move forward?"

He texted the guys a photo of the plan. Hold me to this.

Back at the fridge he colored in two squares with the retreat dates and wrote his initials on dinner. They moved money into the new line they'd named together. He emailed the shelter about an intake call.

The house didn't transform overnight. But the air changed.

At dinner he told the kids, "Mom's serving at the shelter on Tuesdays. I'll be on pickups and dinner. We're all in." He asked her at the table, "What else do you need from me to make this work?"—and wrote down her answer.

Headship stayed. It just moved where it belongs: serving first, deciding last, repenting fast. He didn't lose authority; he lost the need to use it to feel big.

He added a quiet line inside the pantry door: Lead by making room. Prove it with calendar and cash.

Then he tried to live it—one choice at a time.

COVENANT FLAME

Headship is not the power to reroute her life
while yours stays comfortable.

If your "leadership" delays, minimizes,
or dilutes her God-given gifts,
it is **not** Christ's leadership.

Don't explain — **repent**.
Put skin on it:
time, money, access, encouragement, outside eyes.

She does not need permission from your pride;
she needs **partnership under Christ.**

The aim isn't control.

It's **oneness** —

a unity strong enough that both callings can bear fruit.

STRIKE POINTS

Husband:

Where have you been saying "not now" on repeat?

Move **one** of her desires forward this week

with a **date**, a **dollar amount**,

and your **tangible help**.

Wife:

What dream have you kept in the "someday" drawer?

Write **one clear sentence**

and bring it to the table **tonight**.

Together:

Choose one guardrail now:

– a budget line in her name

– a calendar block with his initials on kid-duty

– a weekly check-in with a trusted couple

Put one in place before the week ends.

SCRIPTURE STRIKE

"Husbands, love your wives,

as Christ loved the church

and gave Himself up for her."

— *Ephesians 5:25*

"In humility count others more significant than yourselves."
— *Philippians 2:3*

CLOSING ECHO

After Group

The house was still.
A dish or two waited in the sink.
    He set his phone on the counter, face up —
calendar open to the square they'd colored in.
    She stepped beside him
and traced the block with her fingertip,
as if anchoring the promise to the page.
    "Thank you," she said.
    "For what?" he asked — not fishing.
    "For moving when I spoke."
    He nodded.
No speech.
Just a husband who stopped using "be realistic" to stay comfortable
and started using headship to **make room**
for what God placed in his wife.

Chapter 11

Holy Confrontation

When quiet kills what love could heal

A week after small group, the retreat was on the calendar and Tuesday pickups were his. The house felt lighter—budget line set, dates inked. But faithfulness gets tested in new places. Another kind of quiet began to spread. Not about plans now—about pain.

The cabinet shut a little harder than it needed to. Mara's laugh didn't reach her eyes. Words stayed polite—trimmed to what could pass without drawing blood.

Ethan felt the tug to ask, to cross the room, to touch the live wire gently and see where it sparked. Instead, he backed away and called it giving space.

Mara felt the shift too, but her silence was older than the day. It had grown year by year like a root under concrete—after prayers dismissed, confessions turned into leverage, nights where speaking made the room colder. So she turned inward, folded small, and said she was fine.

What could have been corrected began to corrode. They didn't fall apart in a blow. They fractured in quiet.

Peace at any cost isn't peace, Ethan thought, wiping the counter longer than necessary. Each pass only spread water thin, as if he could smear away what he didn't want to name. Silence feels safer than honesty—but it's just delay dressed as wisdom.

The Spirit pressed sharper than his excuses: You weren't called to comfort. You were called to covenant. And covenant doesn't coddle sin.

Silence had its own liturgy—avoid, downplay, pretend not to notice. It promised peace and delivered distance. Houses hardened that way. And hell smiled, because silence protects what it cannot create: real unity.

If love can't speak, it isn't love, the Spirit whispered. If peace depends on silence, it isn't holy.

At the sink, a glass sweated a ring into the counter. Mara watched the circle form—predictable, easy to wipe, certain to return. She held the towel longer than she needed, fingers pressing cotton until her knuckles whitened. The quiet dripped heavier than the faucet, pooling where words used to go.

She prayed first—small, simple. "Lord, let my words mend, not weaponize. Give me courage to love enough to speak, and mercy enough to listen after. Break this silence without breaking us." The kitchen looked the same when she opened her eyes, but the quiet felt thinner, stretched like glass ready to crack.

She found him in the doorway. "When you shut down," Mara said, steady but not sharp, "I feel invisible. I feel like confession is ammunition and my fear is an inconvenience. I don't want to accuse you. I want us to live."

The words knocked air from Ethan's lungs. His thumb traced a nervous circle in his palm. He wanted to nod, change the subject, promise tomorrow. Another truth pressed harder: the quiet is killing us faster than any argument would.

The reflex rose—to defend, to turn pain into an argument he could win. He let it pass.

Holy confrontation is different, he remembered. It starts in prayer. It names sin, not identity. It waits for God's time, not my temper.

Ethan sat so his posture wouldn't tower. "I've been avoiding because I was afraid I couldn't fix it," he said. "I thought quiet would become peace. It didn't. I've made you carry what was mine to face."

Truth without love isn't Christ, the Spirit kept near. Love without truth isn't Christ either.

They moved slow. They said what they saw, not what they suspected. When Mara said, "This is where I felt small," Ethan didn't dissect it with a microscope. When he said, "This is where I felt shamed," she didn't twist the knife. Ownership replaced humiliation. The room didn't get louder. It got clearer.

Marriage isn't safe from conflict, Ethan thought. It's safe for conflict—when love and truth both sit at the table.

By the time the hall light hummed on its timer, the air felt different. Not tidy. Holy. Ethan asked if he could pray, and this time it wasn't a benediction slapped over a mess; it was a door opened to a God who loved them enough to interrupt their decay.

"Jesus," he said, voice unsteady but honest, "teach us to speak like You—full of grace and truth. Show me my plank before I point at her speck. Keep us near while we learn."

Tears came—not as spectacle, but as proof their covenant still had a pulse.

COVENANT FLAME

Real love doesn't choose quiet to keep things calm;
it chooses **truth to keep things alive**.
  Silence trades covenant for comfort.
Holy confrontation trades comfort for **healing**.
  Pray first.
Name your own sin first.
Speak plainly.
Receive humbly.
Stay present.
  Unity isn't the absence of conflict —
it's the presence of **grace and truth in the same room**.

STRIKE POINTS

Husband:
Where have you been calling avoidance "peace"?
Name one place you will **speak in love tonight** —
and write the first sentence now.
  Wife:
When you speak, do your words aim to **restore** or to **win**?
Prepare one clear, gentle sentence,
and one question that invites his heart instead of probing his flaws.

Together:
Adopt one rule for conflict this week:
– pray aloud before starting
– name your own fault first
– forbid sarcasm and scorekeeping
Choose one — and keep it.

SCRIPTURE STRIKE

"Better is open rebuke than hidden love.
Faithful are the wounds of a friend..."
— *Proverbs 27:5–6*

CLOSING ECHO

The Night the Silence Broke

Later the house dimmed to its familiar creaks.
Mara set the towel down.
    Ethan pulled a chair toward her
and turned his whole body — toward, not away.
For a long moment, neither moved.
    "I feel unseen," she said at last.
    He didn't argue.
He nodded — a small motion
carrying more repentance than a speech.

"I didn't want to fail you," he said softly,
"but I think I already did."

They bowed their heads together —
not as a truce,
but as an altar.

When they lifted them,
nothing in the house looked different,
but everything sounded different.
The quiet wasn't hiding anything anymore.
It was **holding** them.

Chapter 12

The Altar Between Us

Sacrifice as the Center of Union - When the fight becomes holy

You will fight. The question isn't if—it's what kind of fight you'll have. Conflict can burn a house down. Under covenant, it can become an altar.

The dishes were still in the sink. A fork leaned against a plate. Somewhere a faucet dripped like a metronome for restraint. The air carried that charged quiet before a storm—too still, too aware of every sound.

They had circled this argument before: money, tone, needs unmet—the sort that returns like weather. Tonight it arrived again, heavy-footed in the hallway.

Mara didn't raise her voice. Ethan didn't withdraw. That was new.

He rubbed his temple the way he always did when he was trying to measure his words. She folded a dish towel, unfolded it again, buying seconds before something sharp slipped out. Both wanted calm. Both knew calm wasn't the same as peace.

They sat on the floor—not because they felt like it, but because they remembered a vow, and the floor felt closer to humility. The tile's chill climbed through thin fabric and made them honest.

"I don't want to win," he said, the words surprising them both. "I want us to make it through."

Something shifted—fragile, but real. Not a solution, a direction.

He'd been calling quiet wisdom, he realized. It wasn't peace; it was a truce with decay.

They breathed—a count to five, then to ten—because the Spirit often speaks quieter than adrenaline. She said what she saw, not what she suspected. He named his sin first, not hers. They spoke at a pace that kept their words from becoming weapons. The house listened.

We aren't failing because we fight, he thought. We fail when we fight like enemies.

He had learned to keep score. She had learned to hoard silence. Both were forms of fear. Both gave hell a seat at the table. Tonight they tried something else.

"You weren't there with me in the budget," she said, gentler than her frustration wanted. "It made me feel alone."

"I blamed you for my anxiety," he answered, the confession like a stiff door scraping open. "I punished you with quiet."

This feeling is real, she admitted—but it makes a terrible lord.

Don't wait to feel safe to forgive, she reminded herself. Don't wait to feel brave to tell the truth. Obedience first. Feelings can learn the tune.

He reached for her hand and didn't force it. She set her palm in his and didn't yank it back. They prayed—awkward, out loud—the kind of prayer that breaks the chokehold precisely because it's halting and sincere.

"Lord, have mercy on us," he said. "We want unity more than victory. Show me my plank before I point at her speck."

Truth without love isn't Christ, he remembered—and love without truth isn't either. Keep both at the table.

They stayed in the room. No strategic door slams. No dramatic exits. When the heat rose, they paused. When the past tried to testify, they reminded it: forgiven things don't get subpoenaed for tonight's trial. When voices edged too sharp, they softened. When one confessed, the other didn't pounce.

You weren't called to be right, he told his pride. You were called to be holy.

By degrees, their chest-tight anger loosened into plain speech. He owned what was his. She owned what was hers. They forgave fully—not the vague "it's fine," but the costly "I release this debt." The tile became an altar—cold, honest—where pride went to die and mercy rose warm as breath.

Forget perfect words, she thought. What we need is a holy posture.

Later, they rinsed plates. Not as truce, but as liturgy—the small chore that says, we are still us. The faucet hissed, the drain swallowed the suds, and the house felt lighter, like a door had been shut to something that had been pacing the hall.

COVENANT FLAME

Covenant doesn't promise you won't clash.
It promises you'll **choose each other again** when you do.

Your fights will either **burn you down or refine you —
altar or ash**.

Build like the world,
and you'll keep score until nothing is left.

Lay it on the altar
and worship through the ache.

Unity, not victory.
Presence, not punishment.
Obedience first; feelings follow.

STRIKE POINTS

Husband:
When conflict rises, do you lead with humility or dominance?
Name the place you will go first — **to the floor, and to prayer**.

Wife:
When you're hurt, do you shut down or press in with gentle truth?
Write a single sentence that names pain **without wounding**.

Together:
Choose one altar-rule for conflict this week:
- pray aloud early
- name your own sin first
- forbid scorekeeping

Pick it tonight and practice it tomorrow.

SCRIPTURE STRIKE

"Be angry and do not sin; do not let the sun go down on your anger, and give no opportunity to the devil."
— *Ephesians 4:26–27*

CLOSING ECHO

The Altar Rebuilt

They still fought sometimes.
Voices rose, then remembered.
Faces tightened, then softened.
But something in the house had changed —
a place on the kitchen floor the Spirit recognized.

When the heat came, they returned there.
Knees on tile.
Hands linked — sometimes shaking.
Words honest and small.

The faucet dripped like a heartbeat.
The floor stayed cold,
but holy things often are.

And the fire that once consumed them
became the light they knelt beside.

Part IV – The Witness

Why Covenant Still Preaches

Chapter 13

Building What Lasts

Constructing Legacy in Faithfulness

You won't drift into covenant. You have to build it.

Rhythm is the backbone of holy endurance.

The house exhaled Monday. Lunchboxes waited by the door like small promises. The bus had already taken its noise with it. Mara stood at the counter, hair pulled up, sleep still soft at the corners of her eyes.

Ethan came in behind her, kissed her shoulder like a habit chosen on purpose, and set a mug by her hand.

"I prayed for you this morning," Ethan said. Not as a report. As a rhythm.

No fireworks. No speeches. Just the scaffolding that keeps a house from tilting.

They had learned the hard way. Once, they chased highs and feared lows, measuring love by the temperature of the room. It worked until it didn't—feelings spiked, feelings sank, and their covenant rode the waves like a small, frightened boat.

Ethan watched the steam curl from Mara's cup. You won't always feel in love, he thought. You won't always want to serve. Emotion is the spark; rhythm keeps the fire lit.

He slipped a note into a lunchbox—I'm with you. Be brave. Mara set her phone on the shelf where all the phones slept at night. Ethan brushed the back of her hand and didn't pull away first.

No grand gestures. Just nails in a frame built to outlast weather.

Love that lasts is love that works, Ethan reminded himself. It confesses. It plans. It shows up—especially when the mood is gone.

Together they'd built a few anchors to make the week stand up straight—liturgy stretched across ordinary time:
• a ten-second prayer before the door opens to the day
• Sabbath that puts the laptops in a drawer and their bodies in the same room on purpose
• "screens sleep in the kitchen," so eyes can rest on faces
• a budget they look at together—not as court and defendant but as co-builders
• touch that doesn't need fireworks to count
• confession that doesn't wait for exposure

This isn't legalism, Mara thought. It's protection.

They didn't do any of it to impress God. They did it because gates left open invite wolves, and they were done feeding what tried to eat them.

Some weeks it all slipped. Babies got sick. Deadlines grew teeth. Sabbath looked like a nap taken in shifts; prayer sounded like a sigh under blankets. Drift found seams.

But when rhythm breaks, covenant doesn't. You rebuild.

Ethan learned to go first: "I dropped the prayer window this week."

Mara learned to answer without tally: "I let hurry make me sharp."

They reset small things—phones back in the basket, dinner at the table even if it was eggs, a walk down the street without talking about schedules, only noticing the same sky.

The difference between a broken marriage and a lasting one is not failure. It's whether the rhythm gets rebuilt.

Ethan poured another cup and handed it over. Mara took it and smiled with one corner of her mouth, the morning version of a vow.

The house didn't shine. It held. And holding was holy.

You don't live off a wedding day. You build a rhythm for Tuesday.

***

By noon on Tuesday the plan was already fraying. A call ran long. The pickup line crawled. Dinner turned into a sheet-pan scramble. Ethan caught Mara's eye across the kitchen—two witnesses to the same unraveling—and lifted the broom like a tiny flag of truce.

"Reset?"

"Reset," Mara said. Ten minutes each. Counters cleared. Shoes corralled. Apologies traded like bread. Not tidy—enough.

Wednesday carried their midweek rule: name one weight and one gratitude before bed.

Mara: "Weight—felt behind all day. Gratitude—you texted that verse at lunch."

Ethan touched her ankle under the blanket. The room warmed by degrees.

Thursday night, the budget tried to pick a fight. It always did. They kept the co-builder posture: same side of the table, pens in both hands, one prayer before numbers. Ethan circled a line item and glanced at Mara.

"Is this loving our future selves?"

Mara laughed. "Not really." Truth got lighter when pride stayed outside.

Friday night porch check-in after the kids are down—three questions, same chairs.

Where did we love well this week?

Where did we drift?

What's one concrete step before Sunday night?

Ethan set an alarm to cover Saturday errands so Mara could nap. Mara added "text your brother" under Ethan's oil-change reminder. Little braces on a healing bone.

Once a month they added a slow ritual: coffee out, notebooks open, no crisis allowed. They called it "windows and walls." What windows had God opened—places to see and breathe? What walls needed building—boundaries to keep love in and hurry out? Three lines and a date under each. No twelve-point plan. Just a next faithful step with a day attached.

On a night when the week had taken more than it gave, Ethan plugged in both phones on the kitchen shelf and went looking for Mara. No speeches. Just presence. She set her head on his shoulder and listened to the dishwasher hum a benediction.

"We're not impressive," Mara said.

"No," Ethan answered, "but we're here."

And "here," held over time, felt like worship.

Saturday morning, the kids thundered down the hall. Ethan reached for Mara's hand across the pillows and prayed their ten-second prayer out loud—the shorthand for everything they meant by forever.

"Lord, keep us simple and faithful. Help us show up for each other. Guard our house from hurry and from pride."

"Amen," Mara whispered, and the day opened like a door to the same old hall, made new by how they would walk it.

By Sunday, the house didn't look curated. It looked lived-in and kept. The week hadn't been flawless. It had been held. And holding—on purpose, in pattern—was how ordinary days became a legacy.

COVENANT FLAME

The strongest marriages don't burn bright every day;
they endure because they've built something **larger than emotion**.
    Rhythm is the scaffolding of covenant—
how you show up when tired,
how you keep going when numb,
how you fight drift before it becomes distance.
    Don't wait for a feeling.
Build a pattern.
Let the feeling learn the pattern's song.

STRIKE POINTS

Husband:
Which holy rhythm did you abandon, and what single step restores it this week?

Wife:
Which gate has gone unguarded—screens, stress, speech, or friendships?
Name it, and close it gently but firmly.

Together:
Choose one rhythm to rebuild now:
– the ten-second prayer at the door
– Sabbath hours marked in ink
– phones that sleep in the kitchen
Hold it for **four weeks**.

SCRIPTURE STRIKE

"Let us not grow weary in doing good, for in due season we will reap,
if we do not give up."
— *Galatians 6:9*

CLOSING ECHO

The Quiet Return

They lost the rhythm for a while.
Work grew loud.
Kids grew louder.
Small sins slipped in wearing ordinary clothes.
   Then one evening, she reached for his hand without preface.
He clicked the phone to sleep and slid it onto the shelf.
Their fingers laced.
   "Before we make dinner," he said,
"can we thank Him?"

It wasn't polished.
It barely lasted a breath.

But heaven heard the sound of construction—
nails in old wood, a frame finding square again.

And the house, almost imperceptibly,
stood straighter.

Chapter 14

Covenant Under Fire

Enduring When the World Watches

When the storm hits, what's built on emotion collapses. Covenant can preach through the fire.

The sound found them at 3:11 a.m.—not thunder, a train where no tracks ran. The house took a breath it couldn't hold.

Ethan sat up so fast his ribs protested. Mara was already awake, listening for the roof the way a mother listens for a child. Pressure pressed the walls. The window over the dresser bowed once, twice—then shattered inward. Night and rain and glass flew into the room. Ethan moved before he thought, turning his body into the blow. The glass cut his forearm, bright and clean. The bedroom door shuddered; hinge screws tore from the jamb and the door slammed crooked against the frame.

"Bathroom," Mara said, low and steady, and they moved—bare feet on grit, shoulders braced against a wind that wanted inside.

They shut themselves in the small room at the house's center, backs to the tub, towels shoved against the threshold to slow the water's fingers. Mara wrapped a hand towel around his arm, then another, cinched them with a belt. Blood seeped anyway, warm and honest.

"You'll need stitches," she whispered.

"Later," Ethan said. "We hold here for now."

The wind clawed at the siding again. A picture frame hit the hallway floor and broke somewhere beyond the door. They both flinched.

They waited. Five minutes? Ten? The clock had no meaning here. The dark pressed close; the air smelled of wet drywall and iron.

He tried to hear the rise and fall that would tell him the worst had passed. It didn't come. Another gust hit, harder than the rest, and the lights blinked out.

"Still with me?" she asked.

"I'm here."

After that, the words stayed small—just enough to keep fear from having the last sound.

They prayed in fragments.

"Protect the house. Don't let it come apart."

"Keep the kids safe where they are," Mara added.

"Don't let go."

Rain moved through the vent like breath. Shingles lifted; wood groaned; something loose whistled in the yard. Ethan reached for Psalm 46: "Therefore we will not fear though the earth gives way..." His voice failed on the third line, and Mara finished it for him.

Between gusts they whispered memories—small buoys in black water.

"The trip to Asheville."

"The baby's first laugh."

"The way the tree lights reflected on the ceiling that one Christmas."

He laughed once, short, surprised. "I can't believe I'm thinking about the tree right now."

"Maybe that's the point," she said. "To remember what's worth rebuilding."

Minutes slid into one another. The belt around his arm darkened. Her legs cramped from how she sat. They didn't move. When she felt herself start to tremble, he shifted until his shoulder touched hers—just enough weight to say I'm still here.

Outside, another window shattered. The sound came like punctuation.

"I hate this," she said.

"I know."

"I want it over."

"Me too."

"Then why am I calm?"

He exhaled through his teeth. "Maybe because He's actually here."

That thought stayed longer than the thunder.

By gray dawn the wind was a tired animal. They opened the door into a hallway sown with glass. Another interior door hung crooked, hinge screws torn clean from wood. Rain had found the studs. A gutter lay folded in the yard like a broken arm. The frame stood anyway.

So did they.

Mara rinsed his cut at the kitchen sink; the water ran red, then pink, then clear. Ethan kissed her hairline and left a dot of blood on her cheek by mistake.

"Urgent care," she said. "Then we come back and start mending."

On the drive, their hands found each other over the console—bandage rough against her palm, pulse steadying.

Weeks later, the stitches were gone, but his finger still wouldn't close all the way. The doctor called it scar shortening. Mara called it a reminder. When he laced his fingers through hers, one knuckle stayed a breath above the others—a small space that spoke of the night he turned into the glass to shield her.

Suffering didn't find strangers that night. It found a husband and wife who had already decided, on quieter nights, what they would do when wind asked hard questions: cling to God, run toward each other, keep vows speaking when nerves wanted to quit.

You don't walk out of fire unmarked. You walk out unbroken.

COVENANT FLAME

You will suffer. But suffering is not the end; it is the proving ground. Covenant is what you grip when your body shakes, your heart breaks,
and hope runs thin.

Emotion may vanish.

Passion may flicker.

The vow still stands.

The fire does not annihilate covenant—

it reveals the King who stands in it with you.

STRIKE POINTS

Husband:

When the storm hits, do you reach for control, silence, or surrender?
Name it—and choose **surrender**.

Wife:

When hope thins, do you run into fear, into blame, or into the Lord?

Choose the Lord, and say it aloud.

Together:

Name one storm you've survived.

What did it reveal about your frame—

and what one obedience will strengthen it now?

SCRIPTURE STRIKE

"When you walk through fire, you shall not be burned,

and the flame shall not consume you.

For I am the LORD your God..."

— *Isaiah 43:2–3*

CLOSING ECHO

The Fire That Preached

Cleanup took weeks.

Tarps learned their own small hymn over the roofline.

A contractor eyed the missing panes, the chewed siding, the ripped-out screws,

and said, "Could've been worse," and they knew what he meant.

Stitches itched.

The bandage came off.

A thin red seam traced his forearm—sharp as a line drawn by truth.

They stood in the yard when the last tarp came down.

The house wasn't what it had been.

Neither were they.

The wind had taken things.

It had left a testimony.

He touched the scar with the thumb she had steadied in the night.

"We'll see this every day," she said.

"Good," he answered. "Let it preach."

They were still standing—

not because they were unhurt,

but because the vow held when everything else shook.

And the scar, like the house, told the story true.

Chapter 15

This Marriage Preaches

Proclaiming Gospel Through Union

Y our marriage is not private.

It declares something about God.

The only question is what sermon it's preaching.

They slipped in a few minutes late and took the end seats near the double doors. She set the baby carrier on the floor and rocked it with the edge of her shoe. He tried not to think about the checking account or the late notice folded in his pocket like a dare. They hadn't fought on the way here; they hadn't said much either.

During the second song, the back row came into view—the older couple who always sat there. He stood when the room stood. He still opened the hymnal for both of them, though the words were on the screen. When he lifted his arm, a thin scar showed along his forearm; one finger didn't curl all the way. His wife's hand found that arm, quick and familiar—the way you touch something you've decided to be grateful for.

Her husband leaned close. "Is that the couple you told me about?" She nodded. "Back row. Every week."

The sermon was on patience. Her mind wandered in honest places anyway: the half-finished conversation from Thursday, the way he'd gone quiet when she asked for help with the evening routine, the small sting she carried to sleep. The preacher said endurance was ordinary faithfulness stretched over time. She watched the older woman's shoulders and wondered, *How do you get that kind of rest in a room like this?*

The older man's hand found his wife's during prayer—not a squeeze, just steady. She tried to remember the last time they'd held hands in church. She couldn't.

Staying isn't the same as settling, she thought. *Right?*

Her husband whispered again. "Do you think they've always been like that?"

"No," she said too quickly. "Nobody starts like that."

They both looked down.

After the benediction, people moved toward coffee, doors, and waiting schedules. The older couple didn't rush. They had the unhurried way of people who know exactly where they sit. They aimed for the small table near the side exit—the one with the wobbly leg shimmed by folded bulletins.

The young couple lingered in the aisle.

He said, "We should—"

She said, "Maybe just ask—"

Then neither moved.

The older woman looked up and caught her eye. Not dramatic—just a soft lift of the chin: *If you want to talk, we're here.* Something in Lena's chest loosened. She touched Micah's elbow. They steered the stroller toward the table.

"Hi," she said, smaller than she meant. "We see you back here every week."

The older man smiled like that was the most normal sentence in the world. Up close, the scar was a clean seam; the shortened finger more obvious as he steadied the wobbly table.

"We're glad you came over," the older woman said. "I'm Mara. This is Ethan."

"I'm Lena," she said, then laughed at her own nerves. "And this is Micah. And this is... the only child who slept last night." She tapped the carrier.

They all smiled the tired smile parents use.

Micah slid his hands into his pockets. "We're fine," he said—then shook his head. "No. We're not falling apart, but... we're not sure how to stay."

Mara nodded once, slow—like she'd heard that line in a dozen forms. "Coffee?"

They sat. Micah was still choosing words, so Lena went first.

"We don't yell much," she said. "But we drift. Bills, naps, scrolling. I look up and it's like we've been roommates for three days."

Ethan turned his cup in his palm—the way men do when they're trying not to preach. "We didn't drift to here," he said quietly. "We built it. We failed loud sometimes. We repented louder." He glanced at his wife. "We kept a few small things that outlast moods."

"What small things?" Micah asked, before courage could evaporate.

Mara counted on her fingers. "Ten seconds of prayer at the door before work. Phones sleep in the kitchen. Sabbath hours on the calendar—even if it's a walk and eggs for dinner. If it's tense, we sit on the floor to talk—it keeps voices down."

Ethan added, "Tell the truth about your part first. And if you can't fix it now, say that—then do the next right small thing together anyway."

Lena felt a cry rise and pressed it down—not distrust, just the social cost of crying in public. "We're not... broken," she said. "We just don't want to wake up ten years from now as strangers who go to the same church."

Mara's hand lifted an inch, hovered, then settled. "You don't have to be broken to need help. You just have to be human."

Micah said, "We keep waiting to feel like doing the right things."

Ethan smiled without mockery. "Don't. Build the right things. Feelings catch up to the pattern you practice. Sometimes later than you wish—but they do."

Lena's glance dropped to Ethan's forearm. He noticed and rolled the sleeve—honest, not performative.

"Storm night," he said. "Window blew in. I moved too slow to be wise, fast enough to catch the edge." He flexed his hand; one finger stopped just shy of the palm. "Healed fine. Doesn't bend all the way. It reminds me that covering costs something."

"It reminds me that he's here," Mara said—like she'd said it before and meant it every time.

Lena thought of their own Thursday—her at the sink, him in the doorway, both working so hard not to make anything worse that they didn't make anything better. She saw Micah notice the shortened finger, then look away—embarrassed by the intimacy of another man's scar.

Mara rescued them gently. "What's one small thing you could hold this week? Not five. One."

Micah surprised himself. "Ten seconds before I leave for work. We'll pray—even if the baby's screaming."

Lena nodded. "Phones sleep in the kitchen. Mine grabs me, and I reach for him less."

"Those two will change your house," Ethan said.

"We don't have a big story," Lena blurted. "No tornado. No tragedy."

"Good," Mara said. "Then don't wait for one to teach you. Let the small things do it."

They talked a little longer. Nothing heavy. No secrets. Just normal sentences from people not in a hurry to be impressive. Before they parted, Mara asked, "Can we pray?"

They bowed. Ethan's words didn't run; they walked. "Lord, teach them to stay when it's quiet and when it hurts. Give them simple courage to keep a pattern when feelings are thin. Guard their union from contempt. Make their home safe for truth. Let their marriage tell the truth about You."

"Amen," Micah said—annoyed at the heat in his eyes. He wiped it quickly. Mara pretended not to see.

On the way to the car, Lena kept hold of his sleeve. They didn't talk for the first few minutes. Turning onto their street, she finally said it.

"I want to be like that. Not them—us. Us, older, still together."

"Me too," he said.

"Ten seconds," she said.

"Tonight," he answered. "And phones in the kitchen. I'll get the basket."

The baby slept the whole way—praise God for small mercies. They carried the carrier in and set it by the couch. Micah dug out a basket that had held spare mail and keys. He emptied it and set it on the kitchen shelf.

Lena stood by the back door and waited. He came to her. They didn't lock fingers right away—old habits resist. He reached for her hand with the same hand Ethan had flexed in church and thought, *I'd like my scars to mean something when I'm older. Let them be about love, not silence.*

"Ready?" he asked.

She nodded. "Go."

They prayed the smallest prayer they had.

"Lord, help us," he said.

"Teach us to stay," she said.

"Amen," they said together—and laughed once because it sounded like a line they didn't know they knew.

They put their phones in the basket.

It felt like nothing.

It felt like something.

He touched her shoulder as he passed. She leaned back into his hand like it was a place.

They didn't become the back-row couple that night. Nobody does.

But the house held different, and they both noticed.

COVENANT FLAME

Your marriage is already preaching—
not with microphones,
but with habits.

If you wait for feelings,
you will drift.
If you build rhythms,
you will endure.

Repent faster than you defend.
Pray shorter
and more often.
Tell the truth
about your own part first.
Faithfulness—
not performance—
is the sermon people can actually hear.
You won't preach perfection.
Preach perseverance.
Preach with the way you stay.

STRIKE POINTS

Husband:
What are your habits saying about Christ's headship—
service first,
or comfort first?
Choose one act of service
to repeat daily.
Wife:
What are your habits saying about the Church's strength—
courageous trust,
or quiet resentment?
Choose one sentence of gentle truth
to speak this week.
Together:
If a neighbor watched your home for seven days,
what would they believe about God?

Pick one rhythm to clarify the sermon—
ten-second prayer,
phones in the kitchen,
or a weekly hour without screens—
and hold it for four weeks.

SCRIPTURE STRIKE

"This mystery is profound,
and I am saying that it refers
to Christ and the church."
— Ephesians 5:32

CLOSING ECHO

The Last Sermon

Years from now
they won't remember which Sunday this was
or what the second song was called.
    They'll remember
standing by the back door
with hands that didn't know what to do—
and then doing the small thing anyway.
    They'll remember a basket on a shelf
and the way their house felt quieter
without glowing glass between them.

They'll remember two older faces in the back row—
Mara and Ethan—
a scar that showed when a sleeve slid up,
and the steady way those hands
found each other during prayer.

At a long table on another night,
with too many candles
and kids talking over each other,
someone will ask how it started.

"Ten seconds,"
one of them will say.
"And a basket."

They will laugh,
and mean it.

And the room will understand
that this is how sermons are lived—
one kept vow at a time,
one small prayer at a door,
one ordinary hand
that keeps reaching first.

Epilogue

The Eternal Flame

The vows we keep and the battles we endure are not the end of the story.

Marriage preaches, yes — but even marriage points beyond itself.

Every covenant echoes a greater covenant.

Every altar in our homes traces back to the cross.

Every scar borne in love is gathered into Christ's wounds — the Bridegroom who bled first and loves still.

Earthly covenants are temporary.

Some end in death, some in grief, some in quiet triumph.

But the covenant of Christ does not waver.

His flame does not gutter.

His faithfulness cannot fail.

If your marriage has felt like a battlefield, take courage: it was never meant to be the finish line.

It was always meant to be a signpost — a small flame pointing toward the fire that never dies.

One day the wars will cease.

One day the tears will dry.

One day the Bride will stand whole before her Lord.

And every vow kept in the dark
will be gathered into His light
and called precious.

Until that day, hold fast.
Bear the flame.
Let your covenant preach the faithfulness of the One
who keeps His vows when ours falter.

"The steadfast love of the LORD never ceases;
His mercies never come to an end;
they are new every morning;
great is Your faithfulness."
— Lamentations 3:22–23

And when you see the small scars of your own story —
the words forgiven,
the nights endured,
the hands that kept reaching first —
remember this:

The eternal flame still burns.
And Christ's covenant
will never
be broken.

Call to Action

Fan the Flame Together

You have read the stories.

You have seen what covenant can endure.

Now you step into the real work — not dramatic, not loud, but holy.

You have walked through these pages.

You have seen covenant survive storms, silence, scars, and ordinary days.

If it strengthened your home even a little,

let that strength become seed.

Pass this book to one couple who needs hope.

Leave a copy in your church library.

Give one to a newlywed friend.

Start a small group around it.

Place it quietly in someone's hands who isn't ready to ask for help.

You are not selling something.

You are stewarding something.

The flame is not meant to stay in one house.

It is meant to spread —

slowly, warmly, faithfully —

until homes across the world glow with the quiet fire
of covenant kept.

Let your home preach.

Then let it help another home preach too.

Afterword

Why This Book Was Written

I didn't write this because marriage is easy.
I wrote it because marriage is holy — and holy things deserve to be fought for.

I know the long nights, the misfires, the quiet drift that creeps in unnoticed. I've watched people I love walk through storms that should have broken them — and sometimes storms that did. And I've learned this: **covenant isn't sustained by romance or technique, but by a vow anchored in God's faithfulness.**

I'm not writing from theory.

I'm writing from lived ground — from my own scars and rebuilding, from the slow choosing of my wife when feelings ran thin. That is why these words carry weight. **Real marriages are forged, not found.**

But hear this clearly:

Covenant doesn't only demand; it gives.

On the far side of repentance, there is rest.

On the far side of dying to pride, there is peace that feels like oxygen.

On the far side of small, persistent obedience, there is the quiet joy of being known and still chosen.

There is a sweetness reserved for marriages that walked through fire and refused to run. A steadiness formed in homes where forgiveness has been practiced like craft. A tenderness that blooms where two people decide — again and again — to stay.

I'm not glorifying suffering.

I'm pointing to the reward:

the warmth of unity rebuilt,

the trust that rises like dawn,

the laughter that returns after silence,

the sense that God Himself is mending what once frayed.

Covenant isn't always rescue.

Often it's obedience *before* rescue.

But obedience becomes its own path — and the God who walks it with us brings fruit in season.

If you finished this book feeling weight — good.

The cross carries weight.

But if hope rose beneath that weight — even better.

Hope is the mark of the One who keeps His covenant when ours trembles.

If you're still holding your vow — tired, imperfect, still trying — you're already walking the road where glory grows deep roots.

Stay the course.

There is joy ahead — real joy, lasting joy — shaped by the One who never breaks His promises.

And your marriage, held in His hands, can preach that truth.

Acknowledgements
This book would not exist without the broken.

To the ones who stayed after betrayal.

To the ones who wept on bathroom floors.

To the ones who asked hard questions when everything felt hollow.

You showed us what covenant looks like in the dark. We carried your stories with trembling hands.

To the men who kept showing up when no one clapped — we saw you.

To the women who fought for softness when bitterness would have been easier — we learned from you.

You did more than survive.

You bore witness.

These chapters are stitched with your faithfulness.

To those who pushed us to make this sharper, harder, more honest — thank you for refusing a comfortable gospel.

Your courage honed the edge of every page.

To our families — thank you for grace.

For the hours we vanished into quiet.

For the unprinted moments of covenant you lived beside us that meant more than words.

Above all, to the One who authored covenant and bled to restore it — this is for You.

Written by a husband shaped by covenant — with a wife who walked beside every chapter.

Forged in real fire, offered to those walking through their own.

About the author

The author is a husband learning covenant, a father learning grace, and a craftsman by instinct. His life is built around leading people, solving problems, and making things that last — in the shop, in his home, and in his daily walk with Christ.

He didn't write this book because he had everything figured out. He wrote it because he has felt the battle so many marriages face — including his own — and chose not to look away.

The reflections in these chapters were shaped through years of quiet conversations, late-night prayers, hard lessons, and honest rebuilding with his wife, Kari. Her insight, courage, and presence sit behind every page. They talked through the themes, held the difficult truths up to the light, and sought Christ's way together.

Kirk lives in Minnesota, where he works, worships, raises a family, and keeps learning how to stay — one act of faithfulness at a time.